THE STORY GOES ON

For Martin Strand
and
Aki
—M.M.

Text copyright © 2002 by Aileen Fisher, copyright © 2005 Boulder Public Library Foundation, Inc.

Illustrations copyright © 2005 by Mique Moriuchi

A Neal Porter Book

Published by Roaring Brook Press

Roaring Brook Press is a division of Holtzbrinck Publishing Holdings Limited Partnership,

2 Old New Milford Road, Brookfield, Connecticut 06804.

Distributed in Canada by H. B. Fenn and Company Ltd.

Library of Congress Cataloging-in-Publication Data

Fisher, Aileen Lucia, 1906-2003

The story goes on / by Aileen Fisher ; illustrated by Mique Moriuchi.—1st ed.

p.   cm.

Summary: An illustrated poem about the cycle of life—bug eats plant, frog eats bug,

snake eats frog, hawk eats snake, and so on.

ISBN 1-59643-037-0

1. Food chains (Ecology)—Juvenile poetry.   2. Children's poetry, American.

[1. Food chains (Ecology)—Poetry.   2. American poetry.]   I. Moriuchi, Mique, ill.   II. Title.

PS3511.I7294S76 2004   811'.52—dc22   2003018143

Roaring Brook Press books are available for special promotions and premiums.

For details contact: Director of Special Markets, Holtzbrinck Publishers.

First edition 2005

Book design by Jennifer Browne

Printed in the United States of America

10 9 8 7 6 5 4 3 2 1

AILEEN FISHER

THE STORY GOES ON

Pictures by
MIQUE MORIUCHI

A NEAL PORTER BOOK
ROARING BROOK PRESS
BROOKFIELD, CONNECTICUT

Here is the place
for our tale to begin:
this small patch of earth
with a seed hidden in.

Here's where events
will unroll one by one.
With

quick

drops

of

rain.

With

warm

rays

of sun...

The seed breaks its skin
with nary a sound.
A shoot seeks the air.
A root hugs the ground.

A plant starts to grow
and soon, to be brief,
there's a stalk with a green
little fluttery leaf.

Now enter a bug
who's looking for dinner.

He stops.

Ho! A leaf,

a tender beginner.

He climbs the short stalk
to nibble, not knowing
an enemy lurks
where some grasses are growing.

The enemy squats
in the grass, looking smug,
while the green little leaf
makes a meal for the bug.

And then, in a flash,
with the stealth of a thief,
a frog's sticky tongue
flicks out at the leaf
and snatches a meal . . . .

The bug comes to grief.

Now the frog all the while
is quite unaware
that a snake in the grass
waits patiently there,
eager to swallow
the frog for his dinner.

and the snake is the winner.
It somehow is able
to swallow the frog.

happy to relish
the warmth of the day,
not knowing a hawk
will enter the fray.

With a **swish!**
and a **swoop!**

the hawk flashes down.

It snatches the snake
and flies past the town
with the snake in its claws
and the sun on its crown.

It flies over fields
to its nest in a tree,
but it never arrives . . .

for its eyes fail to see
the farmer who waits
in the shade with his gun.

BANG!

BANG!

all the plans
of the hawk are undone.

It falls to the ground . . .
where a coyote will make
a very good meal
of a hawk and a snake.

Then crows come to peck.

And early that night
beetles called sextons
(before it is light)
will bury what's left
completely from sight.

And then in the soil
made rich in this way
a seed will start sprouting
and growing some day.

With quick drops of rain
and warm rays of sun,
events will unroll
as before, one by one:

a leaf

and a bug,

a frog

and a snake,

a hawk

and a man . . .

What a drama they make!

A coyote,

a sexton

From hither or yon ... what a procession to ponder upon as over and over the story goes on.